Contents

outer dry leaves that cover the entire stalk before slicing the tender heart into thin pieces.

Kaffir Lime (Bergamot)

Rinse the whole kaffir lime *(makroot)* before using the peel. Shred the thin peels to be mixed with curry paste.

The leaves, rinsed and shredded, are added to chili soups or hot salad dishes to heighten their aromatic appeal.

Coriander (Chinese Parsley)

In Thai cooking, coriander *(pak chee)* leaves and roots are used. Coriander, also known as Chinese parsley, is a herb with a strong aroma.

Fresh coriander leaves are widely used in garnishing Thai dishes. When using the roots, rinse thoroughly and pound them. The roots are not meant to be eaten but only to give an aromatic flavour to a dish.

Aromatic Ginger

The finger-shaped aromatic ginger *(krachai)* should be soaked and rinsed thoroughly to clean off the soil. Peel and thinly slice each piece crosswise to be pounded with curry paste. Shred them for chili soups or curry dishes.

Third Edition

YOUR FAVOURITE
THAI
DISHES

Wandee Na Songkhla

YOUR FAVOURITE THAI DISHES
Wandee Na Songkhla

PROJECT DIRECTOR
Clive Wing
Catherine Gordon
Y. Lee

DESIGN
Pimmas Suksri

PHOTOGRAPHY
Akasak Kajonkittiyuth

PRINTER
Darnsutha Press Co., Ltd. Thailand.

Copyright © 2004 2002 1999 1996
3rd Revised Edition 2005

ISBN 974-8369-85-4

For information write to:
BOOKNET CO., LTD.
1173, 1175, 1177, 1179 Srinakharin Road,
Suang Luang, Bangkok 10250, Thailand
Tel : 66-2322-3678 (10 Lines)
Fax : 66-2721-1639
Email: booknet@book.co.th

Shallots

Shallots are fondly called *'small onions'* or *'red onions'* among Thai people. Peel, rinse and coarsely chop for chili paste or slice thinly for chili salad dishes. Do not over-add shallots in soups, or they will spoil the taste.

Garlic

Garlic *(krathiem)* with thick skin is used more extensively in Thai cooking than thin skin varieties because it is more aromatic. Garlic is always peeled and crushed before use and used in nearly every Thai dish.

Balsam Leaves

Balsam leaves *(kraprao)* are mostly used in stir fried meat, seafood or chicken dishes in which chilies or chili paste and garlic are among the important ingredients. Uncooked fresh leaves are sometimes used to garnish stir fried dishes. The leaves are sometimes deep fried to make crispy leaves for garnishing.

Basil Leaves

Basil leaves *(horapa)* have aroma and taste that are distinct from balsam leaves and they are also used in stir fried chili dishes or added to chilli soups. Fresh leaves can be eaten raw with barbecued pork, spring rolls and many other dishes.

Sweet Balsam Leaves

Sweet balsam leaves *(bai mang luk)* are used in a few Thai dishes, for example a soup with a variety of herbs and vegetables, known in Thai as *kaeng lieng*. They are also eaten raw with some curry soups.

Tamarind Paste

Tamarind paste *(makham piak)*, made from pitted and shelled tamarind, should be rinsed before being soaked with a small amount of boiling water for 5-10 minutes. Squeeze the paste and use the liquid. It is used in spicy soups and some chili salad dishes.

Spices

The eight spices commonly used in Thai cooking are pepper, coriander seeds, cumin, mace, cardamom, bay leaves, cloves and cinnamon.

Pepper *(prik thai)*: The most widely used form is white pepper, that is, pepper seeds ground without the skin. Black pepper is not so hot and is more aromatic than white pepper. There is also fresh green pepper-

Spring Rolls

ปอเปี๊ยะทอด

Yield: 4 servings

Filling
10   shrimp, shelled and deveined
1/2   cup (100 g.) ground pork
1/3   cup carrot, grated
1/3   cup bean vermicelli, soaked for
      15 minutes, drained and
      shredded
1/3   cup dried wood ears, soaked for
      15 minutes, drained, stemmed
      and shredded

Garnish
      Chinese lettuce, basil leaves,
      cucumbers

Seasoning
3   tablespoons oyster sauce
1   tablespoon soy sauce
2   tablespoons sugar
1   tablespoon seasoning sauce
1/2   teaspoon ground pepper

Other ingredients
2   cups oil for deep frying
1   egg yolk
20   spring roll wrapping sheets, each
      about 6 inches in diameter

Combine all the ingredients
and mix together well. Add
seasoning and stir. Set aside.

Wrapping and frying
1. Place a portion of the filling on
   the bottom half of each
   wrapping sheet.

2. Fold the top over. Fold the right
   side towards the left and the
   left side towards the right. Roll
   up into a tight roll.
3. Seal with the egg yolk.
4. Deep fry the rolls over medium
   heat until golden brown.
5. Drain and serve. Garnish with
   the vegetables.

Garnish
      Chinese lettuce, basil leaves,
      cucumbers.

Sauce
1/3   cup carrot, shredded
1/3   cup Chinese white radish, shredded
3   red chillies, shredded
7   pickled garlic, finely chopped
3   tablespoons garlic, finely chopped

Seasoning
1   cup vinegar
1 1/2 cups sugar
2   tablespoons salt

1. Mix the shredded chillies, the
   pickled garlic and garlic
   together.
2. Stir the mixture above with the
   vinegar, sugar and salt until
   thick over low heat. Leave to
   cool.
3. Add the carrot and Chinese
   white radish.

*Note: The shredded carrot and Chinese white
radish should be mixed with salt and drained
before mixing with the other ingredients.*

Crispy Noodles

หมี่กรอบ

Yield: 2 servings

1   pack (30 g.) rice noodles
5   cups oil for deep frying
$1/2$ cup bean curd cakes, cut into cubes
$1/4$ cup (70 g.) shrimp, chopped
$1/4$ cup (50 g.) chicken, finely chopped
3   tablespoons shallots, shredded
1   egg, beaten

Seasoning

4   tablespoons palm sugar
2   tablespoons fish sauce
3   tablespoons tamarind juice
$1/2$ teaspoon chilli powder
3   tablespoons tomato sauce

Garnish

Bean sprouts, pickled garlic cloves, shredded chillies, coriander leaves.

Preparation of crispy noodles

1. Soak the rice noodles for 15 minutes and drain.
2. Divide the rice noodles into small portions. Deep fry each portion of the noodles in hot oil until golden brown. Set aside all the fried noodles.
3. Fry the bean curd cakes, shrimp and chicken until fragrant. Set aside.
4. Heat vegetable oil in a pan. Slowly pour the beaten egg little by little into the oil until the egg is crispy. Set aside.

Preparation of the seasoning sauce

Combine the seasoning over low heat, add the shrimp, chicken and shallot. Stir until the sauce is thick.

1. Heat the seasoning sauce over low heat, add the deep fried rice noodles and stir. Add the bean curd and set aside.
2. Transfer to a serving plate. Garnish with the vegetables.

Stuffed Crab

ปูจ๋า

Yield : 2 servings

2   *salted eggs, each yolk cut into half*
¹/₄   *cup (50 g.) crab meat*
¹/₄   *cup (50 g.) ground pork*
3   *eggs*
4   *crab shells*
2   *red chilies, cut lengthwise*
2   *stalks coriander*

Seasoning

2   *tablespoons soy sauce*
1   *teaspoon ground pepper*
¹/₂   *teaspoon sugar*

Preparation

1. Mix the crab meat and ground pork together with one egg and the seasoning.
2. Stuff the crab shells with the mixture.
3. Top each piece with the salted egg yolk. Garnish with coriander and chili strips.
4. Steam the stuffed crab in a steamer for about 30 minutes. Leave to cool.
5. Beat the 2 remaining eggs. Dip the stuffed crab in the beaten egg.
6. Heat the oil over medium heat. Deep fry the stuffed crab until golden brown. Serve hot, crab meat side up, with tomato sauce.

Note: If crab shells are not available, shape the mixture into balls and garnish with the salted egg yolks, coriander leaves and red chilli strips.

Sun-Dried Beef

เนื้อแดดเดียว

Yield: 2 servings

235g. beef, cut into 2-inch pieces
1   cup oil

Seasoning
1   tablespoon oyster sauce
1   tablespoon seasoning sauce
1   teaspoon soy sauce
1/4   teaspoon ground pepper
1   tablespoon oil
3   tablespoons chilli sauce or
    tomato sauce

Garnish
Chinese lettuce and tomatoes

Preparation
1. Marinate the meat with the seasoning for 15-20 minutes.
2. Place the meat on a tray and leave in the sun for 30 minutes.
3. Deep fry the sun-dried meat in medium heat for 10-15 minutes or until golden brown.
4. Drain the oil. Serve with the chili sauce or tomato sauce. Garnish with the vegetables.

Note: Pork may be substituted for beef.

Rice Crackers with Dip

ข้าวตังหน้าตั้ง

Yield : 2 servings

7   pieces of rice crackers
2   cups oil for deep frying

Ingredients for the dip

4   shrimp, shelled and deveined
$^1/_3$ cup (70 g.) ground pork
$^1/_3$ cup roasted peanuts, ground
1   red chilli pepper, cut lengthwise
3   tablespoons shallots, diced
3   tablespoons garlic, finely
     chopped
1   tablespoon coriander

Seasoning

3   tablespoons chilli paste oil
3   tablespoons chilli paste
$^1/_3$ cup tamarind juice
$^1/_3$ cup sugar
2   teaspoons salt
2   cups coconut cream

Preparation of the rice crackers

Heat the oil in a pan. Deep fry
the rice crackers, 4-5 pieces at a
time, until golden brown. Drain
and set aside.

Preparation of the dip

1. Cut the shrimp into small
   pieces.
2. Bring the coconut cream to the
   boil for about 3 minutes.
   Reduce the heat. Add the
   ground pork, shrimp and stir
   until done.
3. Add the garlic, shallots, simmer
   for 10-15 minutes until
   the mixture is thick.
4. Add the seasoning, peanuts,
   chili paste and oil from chilli
   paste. Stir together well.
   Transfer the dip to a bowl and
   sprinkle with the red chili,
   pepper and coriander. Serve
   with the rice crackers.

Shrimp Nuggets

แฮ้กน

Yield : 4 servings

10 (130 g.) shrimp, shelled, deveined and finely chopped
1/2 cup (100 g.) pork fat, diced
1 teaspoon ground pepper
1 teaspoon salt
1/2 teaspoon sugar
3 tablespoons cornflour (cornstarch) or plain flour
2 soy bean sheets
2 eggs
1 tablespoon tapioca flour

Garnish
Chinese lettuce, cucumbers, tomatoes, pineapple

Preparation
1. Combine the shrimp, salt, ground pepper and sugar. Knead the mixture until stiff, add in beaten eggs, pork fat and cornflour (cornstarch). Knead again thoroughly to make the filling.

2. Sprinkle some water on the soy bean sheets to soften them. Cut each sheet into 5 x 8 inches.
3. Place a portion of the filling on a soy bean sheet and roll up tightly. Close the edge with a mixture of tapioca flour in no. 4.
4. Mix the tapioca flour with 1/4 cup of water and stir over low heat until thick. Use the mixture to seal the edges of the shrimp rolls in no. 3.
5. Place the shrimp rolls in a steamer over boiling water and steam for 20 minutes. Transfer from the steamer and leave to cool.
6. Slice the shrimp rolls into 1/2-inch pieces and deep fry in medium hot oil until golden brown. Garnish with vegetables and serve with the sauce for Crab Nuggets on page 25.

Crab Nuggets

ห้อยจ๊อ

Yield : 4 servings

4 cups (300 g.) crab meat
1 cup (150 g.) pork fat, steamed and diced
2 eggs
1½ tablespoons soy sauce
1 teaspoon salt
1 teaspoon ground pepper
½ cup cornflour (cornstarch)

Other ingredients
2 soy bean sheets
2 cups oil for deep frying

Sauce
1½ cups sugar
1 cup vinegar
2 tablespoons salt
2 red chillies, finely pounded
2 teaspoons garlic, finely pounded

Garnish
Tomatoes, cucumbers

Preparation
1. Mix the ingredients to make the filling. Divide the filling in half.
2. Sprinkle some water on the soy bean sheets to soften them.
3. Place one portion of the filling on a soy bean sheet and roll the sheet over the filling. Seal both edges and roll up into a long, tight roll. Use a string or thread to tie the roll 1-inch apart. Wrap the other half of the filling with the other soy bean sheet.
4. Place the crab rolls in a steamer over boiling water and steam for 10 minutes. Remove the rolls from the steamer and leave to cool. Remove the strings. Cut the crab rolls into ½-inch pieces to make nuggets.
5. Deep fry the nuggets in hot cooking oil until golden brown. Drain the nuggets on paper towels.
6. Garnish with vegetables when served with the sauce.
7. Mix the sauce ingredients together to make sweet and sour sauce.

Note: If soy bean sheets are not available, egg sheets may be substituted for the wrapping. To make egg sheets, beat a few eggs until smooth. Place a frying pan over moderate heat and oil the pan lightly. Pour a portion of the beaten eggs into the pan and spread into a thin round sheet. Remove and cool.

Fried Rice with Salted Beef

ข้าวผัดเนื้อเค็ม

Yield : 1 serving

$^1/_2$ cup (60 g.) fried salted beef, shredded
1 tablespoon onion, diced
1 tablespoon tomato, diced
1 tablespoon spring onion, finely chopped
1 tablespoon garlic, finely chopped
1 cup cooked rice
3 tablespoons vegetable oil
1 egg

Garnish
Sliced cucumbers, spring onions and lemon slices.

Seasoning
1 teaspoon sugar
1 tablespoon soy sauce
$^1/_4$ teaspoon ground pepper

Method
1. Heat the vegetable oil in a pan, fry the garlic until fragrant. Add the egg, salted beef and rice, and stir well.
2. Add the onion, tomato and spring onion, stir for 5 minutes. Add the seasoning, stir thoroughly.
3. Transfer the fried rice to a plate and garnish with the vegetables.

Note: Salted beef which is sun-dried is recommended.
- Pork may be substituted for the salted beef.
- If salted beef is unavailable, fresh tenderloin of beef is a good substitute. Slice the beef crossways 2-inch thick, to make up 1 cup. Marinate the beef in a mixture of 1 tablespoon soy sauce, 1 tablespoon oyster sauce, $^1/_4$ teaspoon ground pepper, 1 tablespoon seasoning sauce, 1 teaspoon vegetable oil. Refrigerate. When cooking, deep fry the beef until golden brown.

Fried Rice
with Chicken and Mint Leaves

ข้าวผัดไก่กะเพรา

Yield : 1 serving

¹/₄ cup (50 g.) chicken, finely chopped
2 tablespoons red mint leaves
2 red chillies, sliced
5 tiny chillies, finely chopped
1 teaspoon garlic, finely chopped
3 tablespoons vegetable oil
1 cup cooked rice

Garnish
Sliced cucumbers and lemon slices.

Seasoning
¹/₂ teaspoon fish sauce
¹/₂ teaspoon thick soy sauce
2 tablespoons oyster sauce

Preparation
1. Heat the vegetable oil in a pan, fry the garlic until fragrant. Add the chicken, stir well for 3 minutes then add the seasoning.
2. Add the cooked rice, stir thoroughly.
3. Add the mint leaves and chillies, stir well. Transfer the fried rice to a serving plate, garnish with the sliced cucumbers and lemon slices.

Note:
- *Pork or shrimp may be substituted for the chicken.*
- *Red mint leaves are more fragrant than green mint leaves.*

Fried Rice with Sausage

ข้าวผัดไส้กรอก

Yield : 1 serving

$^1/_4$ cup (50 g.) sausages, diced
1   (30 g.) onion, diced
1   (30 g.) tomato, diced
1   tablespoon spring onion, chopped
3   tablespoons vegetable oil
1   cup cooked rice
1   egg

Garnish

Cucumbers, tomatoes, spring onions and lemon slices.

Seasoning

1   tablespoon soy sauce
1   teaspoon sugar
$^1/_4$ teaspoon ground pepper

Preparation

1. Heat the vegetable oil in a pan, fry the sausages for 3 minutes. Beat the egg and stir in to mix with the sausages. Add the cooked rice, stir well.
2. Add the onion and tomato, stir for 1 minute.
3. Add the seasoning, spring onions and stir well. Garnish with sliced cucumbers, tomatoes, spring onions and lemon slices.

Fried Rice with Shrimp

ข้าวผัดกุ้ง

Yield : 1 serving

1   cup cooked rice
3   (15 g.) fresh shrimp, shelled and deveined
1   (50 g.) onion, diced
1   (40 g.) tomato, diced
1   teaspoon garlic, finely chopped
1   salted egg, fried and cut into 4 pieces (optional)
2   tablespoons shrimp sauce (optional)
3   tablespoons vegetable oil
1   cup vegetable oil (to fry egg)

Garnish
Sliced cucumbers, tomatoes and lemon slices.

Seasoning
1   teaspoon sugar
1   teaspoon seasoning sauce

Preparation

1. Heat the vegetable oil (1 cup) in a pan, fry the salted egg for 5 minutes, set aside.
2. Clean the pan and heat the vegetable oil (3 tablespoons) in the pan. Fry the garlic until fragrant, add the shrimp, stir for 2 minutes. Add the rice, stir for 3 more minutes.
3. Add all the vegetables, stir well for 2 minutes, then add the shrimp sauce (if preferred), seasoning and stir together.
4. Garnish with sliced cucumbers, tomatoes and lemon slices.

Fried Rice with Chinese Sausage

ข้าวผัดกุนเชียง

Yield : 1 serving

1 cup cooked rice
1/4 cup (50 g.) Chinese sausages, fried and diced
1 tablespoon spring onion, chopped
3 tablespoons vegetable oil
1 egg
1 teaspoon garlic, finely chopped

Seasoning

1 tablespoon soy sauce
1/2 teaspoon dark soy sauce
1/4 teaspoon ground pepper
1 teaspoon sugar

Garnish

Sliced cucumbers, spring onions and lemon slices.

Preparation

1. Heat the oil in a pan, fry the garlic until fragrant, add the Chinese sausages and egg. Stir well.
2. Add the rice to the pan, stir for 3 minutes then add the seasoning.
3. Stir together well, mix in the spring onion and remove to a dish. Garnish with a variety of vegetables.

Fried Rice with Thai Sausage

ข้าวผัดแหนมสด

Yield : 1 serving

1   cup cooked rice
1/4 cup (50 g.) Thai sausages, sliced
1   tablespoon spring onion,
     chopped
1   egg
3   tablespoons oil
1   teaspoon garlic, finely chopped

Seasoning

1   tablespoon soy sauce
1   teaspoon sugar
1/2 teaspoon ground pepper

Garnish

Sliced cucumbers, tomatoes,
lemon slices and spring onions.

Preparation

1. Heat the oil in a pan, fry the
   garlic until fragrant, add the
   egg and Thai sausages. Stir for
   3 minutes.
2. Add the rice, stir together, add
   the seasoning and spring onion.
   Stir well and remove to a dish.
   Garnish with the vegetables.

Pan-Fried Noodles with Pork and Asparagus

ผัดซีอิ๊วหมูหน่อไม้ฝรั่ง

Yield : 1 serving

1   cup (80 g.) rice noodles
1/2 cup asparagus, cut into 1-inch
     pieces
1/2 cup (100 g.) pork, thinly sliced
1   egg
3   tablespoons oil

Seasoning

1   teaspoon fish sauce
2   teaspoons soy sauce
1   tablespoon sugar
1/2 teaspoon ground pepper

Preparation

1. Heat the oil in a pan, stir in the
   pork, add the asparagus and
   noodles. Stir for 5 minutes.
2. Add the seasoning sauce and
   the egg. Stir for 3 more
   minutes. Serve hot.

Note:
*Chinese broccoli may be substituted for the
asparagus. Shrimp or chicken may be
substituted for the pork.*

Pan-Fried Noodles with Chicken

ก๋วยเตี๋ยวไก่ชาววัง

Yield : 1 serving

1 cup (80 g.) rice noodles
1/2 cup (100 g.) chicken, thinly sliced
3 tablespoons oil
1 teaspoon garlic, finely chopped
1 lettuce

Seasoning

1 teaspoon fish sauce
2 teaspoons soy sauce
1/2 teaspoon thick soy sauce
1 tablespoon sugar
1/2 teaspoon ground pepper

Preparation

1. Heat the oil in a pan. Fry the garlic until fragrant.
2. Add the chicken and stir for 5 minutes until the chicken is cooked. Add the rice noodles, stir well for 2 minutes.
3. Pour in the seasoning sauce and stir fry.
4. Serve hot on a bed of shredded lettuce.

Noodles Fried with Spicy Chicken

ก๋วยเตี๋ยวผัดขี้เมาไก่

Yield : 1 serving

1   *cup (80 g.) rice noodles*
$^{1}/_{2}$ *teaspoon thick soy sauce*
4   *tablespoons vegetable oil*
$^{1}/_{2}$ *cup (100 g.) chicken breast,*
      finely chopped
1   *teaspoon chillies, pounded*
1   *teaspoon garlic, finely chopped*
20   *basil leaves*
$^{1}/_{2}$ *cup chicken broth*

Seasoning

1   *teaspoon fish sauce*
1   *tablespoon sugar*
2   *teaspoons soy sauce*

Preparation

1. Heat 1 tablespoon of the oil in a pan. Fry the noodles and thick soy sauce together for 3 minutes. Transfer to a plate and set aside.

2. Heat the remaining 3 tablespoons of oil in a pan. Fry the garlic and chillies until fragrant. Stir in the chopped chicken breast.

3. Pour in the broth, bring to a boil and add the basil leaves. Before serving, top the noodles with the chicken mixture. Serve hot.

Tom Yam Shrimp Noodle Soup

ก๋วยเตี๋ยวต้มยำกุ้ง

Yield : 1 serving

1　cup (80 g.) rice noodles
1/2　cup (200 g.) shrimp, shelled and deveined
2　stalks lemongrass
3　bergamot leaves
1　teaspoon chilies, pounded
5　mushrooms, halved or quartered
2　tablespoons coriander leaves
1　cup broth

Seasoning
1　tablespoon fish sauce
1　tablespoon lemon juice
1　tablespoon sugar
1/2　teaspoon ground pepper

Preparation
1. Boil the noodles in boiling water for 2 minutes. When done rinse with cool water. Drain and set aside.
2. Heat the broth until it boils, add the shrimp, lemongrass, bergamot leaves, chilies, mushrooms and continue boiling for 5 minutes.
3. Add the seasoning.
4. Transfer the boiled noodles into a bowl. Pour the shrimp soup over the noodles. Sprinkle with coriander. Serve hot.

Pan-Fried Spicy Noodles

ก๋วยเตี๋ยวคั่วหมู

Yield : 1 serving

1   cup (80 g.) rice noodles

1   cup (80 g.) rice noodles
1/2   cup (100 g.) pork
2   tablespoons tomato, sliced
     lengthwise
2   tablespoons onion, cut
     lengthwise
2   tablespoons string beans or peas,
     cut into 1-inch pieces
20   mint leaves
1   teaspoon garlic, chopped
1   teaspoon chillies, pounded
3   tablespoons vegetable oil

Seasoning
1/2   teaspoon thick soy sauce
1   teaspoon fish sauce
1   tablespoon sugar
2   tablespoons tomato sauce
1/2   teaspoon ground pepper

Preparation
1. Heat the oil in a pan. Fry the garlic and chillies for a few minutes.
2. Add the pork, stir fry for 5 minutes, add the tomato and onion slices and peas, stir well.
3. Add the noodles, stir for 3 minutes.
4. Stir in the seasoning sauce and mint leaves. Serve hot.

Phat Thai Kung Sod

(Fried Noodles with Fresh Shrimp)

ผัดไทยกุ้งสด

Yield : 1 serving

1/2 cup (15 g.) preserved small rice noodles, soaked in water
1/3 cup bean sprouts
1 tablespoon garlic chives, cut into 1-inch pieces
1 tablespoon dried shrimp, deep-fried
1 tablespoon sweet pickled radish, chopped
3 tablespoons oil
3 (15 g.) fresh shrimp, shelled and deveined
1 egg
1 tablespoon peanuts, crushed
1 tablespoon bean curd, cut into 1/2-inch cubes

Garnish

Bean sprouts, lime, garlic chives

Seasoning

1 tablespoon fish sauce
1 teaspoon lime juice
1 tablespoon tomato sauce
2 tablespoons sugar
1 teaspoon chilli sauce
1/3 cup water
1 teaspoon chilli powder

Preparation

1. Heat the oil in a pan. Add the fresh shrimp, bean curd, and noodles. Stir well for 3 minutes and add the water. Stir until the noodles are tender.
2. Add the seasoning, bean sprouts and garlic chives. Beat in the egg and add the dried shrimp and peanuts. Stir well and serve hot. Garnish with the bean sprouts, garlic chives and halved lime.

Note:
- *Tamarind juice may be substituted for the lime juice.*
- *Pork and chicken may be substituted for the shrimp.*
- *Do not over-stir the noodles.*

Fried Noodles with Shrimp, Vegetable and Gravy

ก๋วยเตี๋ยวราดหน้ากุ้ง

Yield : 1 serving

1 cup (80 g.) rice noodles
5 (65 g.) shrimp
1/2 cup asparagus, cut into 1-inch pieces
1 tablespoon cornflour (cornstarch)
11/2 cups broth
1 tablespoon oil
1/2 teaspoon thick soy sauce
1/4 teaspoon ground pepper

Seasoning
2 tablespoons soy sauce
1 teaspoon soy bean
1 tablespoon oyster sauce
1 tablespoon sugar

Chili vinegar (optional)
Mix one tablespoon of diagonally-cut red, green or yellow chilies with 2 tablespoons of vinegar.

Preparation
1. Heat the oil in a pan, stir in the noodles. Add the thick soy sauce, stir until the noodles are tender. Set aside.
2. Pour the broth into a pan, add the shrimp and asparagus, cook for 3 minutes or until boiled.
3. Add the seasoning. Dissolve the cornflour in a small amount of water and pour into the broth. Bring the gravy to the boil.
4. Put the cooked noodles in a dish and pour the gravy on top of the noodles. Sprinkle with the ground pepper.

Note:
- *Chinese broccoli may be substituted for the asparagus.*
- *Different kinds of meat may be substituted for the shrimp.*

Spiced Seafood and Meat Salad

ยำรวมมิตร

Yield: 2 servings

1   (5 g.) shrimp, shelled and deveined
3   (5 g.) squid, cut into 1 x 2-inch pieces
3   pieces (5 g.) thinly sliced pork
3   pieces (5 g.) thinly sliced chicken breast
3   pieces (5 g.) thinly sliced beef
1   celery stalk, cut into 1-inch pieces
1   tablespoon chillies, pounded
2   tablespoons onion, slice lengthwise
2   tablespoons tomato, cut lengthwise Chinese lettuce to garnish

Seasoning
2   tablespoons fish sauce
1   teaspoon sugar
2   tablespoons lemon juice

Preparation

1. Bring water to the boil, parboil all the meat for 3 minutes. Drain and place in a bowl.
2. Mix the vegetables and seasoning in the bowl of cooked meats.
3. Transfer the salad to a serving plate and arrange the Chinese lettuce around the edge of the plate.

Note:
Some meats may be omitted, if preferred.

Bean Vermicelli Salad

ยำวุ้นเส้น

Yield : 2 servings

1	small package (20 g.) bean vermicelli, soaked and drained
2	(10 g.) shrimp, shelled and deveined
1/4	cup (50 g.) minced pork
1	tablespoon dried shrimp, deep fried
1	celery stalk, cut into 1-inch pieces
2	tablespoons shallots, cut lengthwise
2	cups water

Garnish
5   Chinese lettuce leaves
1   tomato

Seasoning
1   tablespoon fish sauce
1   teaspoon sugar
1   tablespoon lemon juice

Preparation
1. Bring the water to the boil. Parboil the bean vermicelli, pork and shrimp. Drain and transfer to a bowl.
2. Thoroughly mix other ingredients into the bowl of bean vermicelli, pork and shrimp. Add the seasoning.
3. Serve on a bed of shredded Chinese lettuce and sliced tomato.

Fried Fish and Mango Salad

ยำมะม่วงปลาสำลี

Yield : 2 servings

1   *(150 g.) whole fish*
¹/₄   *cup (150 g) peeled mango, finely shredded*
¹/₄   *cup peanuts, roasted*
3   *tablespoons shallots, thinly sliced*
4   *cups vegetable oil*

Seasoning
2   *tablespoons fish sauce*
3   *tablespoons sugar*
2   *tablespoons lemon juice*
1   *tablespoon chilies, finely chopped*

Method
1. Slice the fish along the belly, clean and rinse thoroughly. Score the fish by making a few diagonal slashes on each side. Deep fry the fish in hot oil until golden brown.
2. Mix the seasoning in a small bowl, add mango, peanuts and shallots.
3. Transfer the fish to a serving plate. When served, the seasoning mixture may be poured on top of the fish or served separately.

Spiced Beef Salad

ยำเนื้อย่าง

Yield : 2 servings

½ cup (100 g.) beef
1 (70 g.) onion
1 cucumber
1 tomato
1 celery stalk, cut into 1-inch pieces
1 tablespoon chillies, pounded

Garnish
3 Chinese lettuce leaves
1 cucumber
1 tomato

Seasoning
1 tablespoon fish sauce
1 teaspoon sugar
1 tablespoon lemon juice

Preparation
1. Grill the beef over medium-low heat for 10 minutes. Cut into thick chunks of ½ x 2 inches and set aside.
2. Mix all the ingredients thoroughly with the beef.
3. Garnish with the Chinese lettuce, sliced cucumber and sliced tomato.

Note:
Pork may be substituted for beef.

Catfish Flake Salad

ยำปลาดุกฟู

Yield: 2 servings

2 (150 g.) fresh catfish
1/4 cup (150 g.) peeled green mango, finely shredded
1 tablespoon chillies, finely chopped
1/4 cup peanuts, roasted
3 tablespoons shallots, thinly sliced
4 cups oil

Seasoning
3 tablespoons fish sauce
3 tablespoons sugar
3 tablespoons lemon juice

Preparation
1. Grill the catfish, leave to cool. Scrape the meat off the fish and chop the fish meat into flakes. Deep fry the fish flakes in medium hot oil.
2. Transfer the fish flakes to one side of a serving dish. Decorate the other side with the other ingredients.
3. Mix the seasoning and pour over the dish when served.

Spicy Shrimp Salad

กุ้งพล่า

Yield : 2 servings

10 shrimp, shelled and deveined
1 tablespoon lemongrass, finely chopped
1 tablespoon Thai parsley, finely chopped
1 tablespoon shallots, sliced lengthwise
1 tablespoon spring onion, finely chopped
1 teaspoon chilli powder
15 mint leaves
1 teaspoon kaffir lime leaves, shredded

Seasoning
2 tablespoons fish sauce
2 tablespoons lemon juice
1 teaspoon sugar
1 tablespoon chilli paste

Garnish
Chinese lettuce, tomato slices

Preparation
1. Stir fry the shrimp in a pan for about 1 minute. Leave to cool.
2. Mix the shrimp and the remaining ingredients in a bowl.
3. Add all the seasoning, mix together well.
4. Put the mixture on a bed of lettuce and garnish with tomato slices. Sprinkle with a few mint leaves.

Spicy Beef/Pork Salad

(Lap Neua/Mu)

ลาบเนื้อ/หมู

Yield : 1 serving

¼   cup (50 g.) ground beef or pork
2   stalks Thai parsley, finely chopped
1   tablespoon spring onions, finely chopped
1   tablespoon shallots, finely chopped
½   teaspoon chili powder
15   mint leaves
1   tablespoon rice, roasted and ground
½   cup stock

Fresh vegetables for a side dish

Cabbage, string beans, spring onions, sweet basil leaves.

Seasoning

1   tablespoon lemon juice
1   tablespoon fish sauce
¼   teaspoon sugar

Preparation

1. Bring the stock to a boil, stir in the meat until done and the stock is dry. Set aside.
2. Mix the remaining ingredients with the meat.
3. Add all the seasoning and transfer to a serving dish. Serve separately with the fresh vegetables.

Green Papaya Salad

ส้มตำไทย

Yield: 2 servings

1   cup (70 g.) green papaya, coarsely granted or julienned
3   cherry tomatoes, halved
2   string beans, cut into 1-inch pieces
1   tablespoon roasted peanuts
1   tablespoon dried shrimp
5   red chillies
5   cloves garlic

Serving vegetables
1   piece red cabbage
1   piece white cabbage
2   string beans
10   stalks water spinach

Seasoning
1   tablespoon fish sauce
1   tablespoon palm sugar
1   tablespoon lemon juice

Preparation
1. In a mortar, coarsely pound the chillies and garlic.
2. Add the string beans, cherry tomatoes and pound lightly.
3. Add the dried shrimp, peanuts and the seasoning.
4. Add the papaya and pound everything together. Serve with the vegetables.

Note:
For Green Papaya Salad with Salted Field Crab, substitute the dried shrimp with a salted field crab.

Thick Curry with Pork

พะแนงหมู

Yield : 3 servings

3   tablespoons thick (panaeng) curry paste
1   cup (200 g.) pork, thinly sliced
1/2   cup thick coconut cream
1/2   cup coconut milk
3   kaffir lime leaves, shredded
2   red chillies, cut lengthwise
1/2   cup basil leaves

Seasoning
2   tablespoons fish sauce
2   tablespoons sugar

Preparation

1. Bring the coconut milk to the boil, add the pork and simmer over low heat for about 5 minutes, set aside.
2. Heat the coconut cream in a pan, stir in the panaeng curry until fragrant (about 3 minutes). Add the seasoning.
3. Add the kaffir lime leaves, chillies, basil leaves, bring to the boil and immediately transfer from the heat.
4. The two pans (step 1 & 2) must be combined at the same point.

Note:
Chicken or beef may be substituted for the pork.

Green Curry with Shrimp

แกงเขียวหวานกุ้ง

Yield : 3 servings

2   *tablespoons green curry paste*
7   *(100 g.) shrimp, shelled and deveined*
1¹/₂ *cups (360 g.) coconut milk*
5   *round eggplants (cut each into 4-6 pieces)*
4   *green and red chillies, cut lengthwise*
¹/₂ *cup basil leaves*
3   *kaffir lime leaves, shredded*

Seasoning

1   *tablespoon fish sauce*
¹/₂ *tablespoon sugar*

Preparation

1. Bring 1 cup of the coconut milk to the boil, stir in the green curry paste and stir continuously for about 5 minutes or until fragrant.
2. Add the shrimp, round eggplants and cook. Add the seasoning and the remaining coconut milk.
3. Add the chillies, basil leaves and kaffir lime leaves. Serve hot.

Note:

In addition to curries, basil leaves are also recommended for various stir fried spicy dishes.

Roast Duck Curry

แกงเผ็ดเป็ดย่าง

Yield : 3 servings

2   tablespoons red curry paste
1   cup (300 g.) roast duck, cut
     diagonally
1¹/₂ cups coconut milk
3   cherry tomatoes
¹/₂ cup tiny eggplants (optional)
2   red chillies, cut lengthwise
¹/₂ cup basil leaves
3   kaffir lime leaves, shredded

Seasoning
2   tablespoons fish sauce
1   tablespoon sugar

Preparation
1. Bring 1 cup of coconut milk to
   the boil, add the red curry paste
   and stir for 5 minutes or until
   fragrant.
2. Add the roast duck, bring to the
   boil again.
3. Add the cherry tomatoes, tiny
   eggplants and simmer. Stir in
   the seasonings and ¹/₂ cup of
   the coconut milk.
4. Add chillies, basil leaves, kaffir
   lime leaves and bring to the
   boil again. Transfer from the
   heat.

Note:
Pork or grilled beef may be substituted for the
roast duck.

Tom Yam Kung

(Hot and Spicy Shrimp Soup)

ต้มยำกุ้ง

Yield : 2 servings

10   (200 g.) shrimp, shelled and deveined
1   stalk lemongrass, cut length-ways
1   piece galangal, thinly sliced
3   kaffir lime leaves, shredded
1   tablespoon chillies, coarsely pounded
$^1/_2$ cup (70 g.) straw mushrooms, halved
2   tablespoons coriander leaves
$1^1/_2$ cups stock

Seasoning
2   tablespoons fish sauce
2   tablespoons lemon juice

Preparation
1. Bring the stock to the boil, add the shrimp.
2. Add the mushrooms, lemon-grass, galangal and kaffir lime leaves into the boiling stock for 5 minutes. Add the seasoning and chillies.
3. Garnish with coriander. Serve hot.

Note:
Another tablespoon of pounded chilies may be added to the soup, if preferred.

Hot and Sour Beef Soup

ต้มยำเนื้อ

Yield : 3 servings

½ cup (100 g.) beef, thinly sliced
7 pieces galangal, thinly sliced
1 stalk lemongrass, cut
   lengthways into 1-inch pieces
3 kaffir lime leaves, shredded
1 tablespoon chillies, coarsely
   pounded
3 celery leaves, finely chopped
1 teaspoon chilli powder
2 cups chicken stock
1 tablespoon coriander for
   garnishing

Seasoning
3 tablespoons fish sauce
3 tablespoons lemon juice

Preparation

1. Bring the chicken broth to the
   boil. Add the beef and
   simmer for 20 minutes.
2. Add the remaining ingredients
   and the seasoning.
3. Serve hot in a bowl. Garnish
   with coriander.

Note :
*Other kinds of meat may be substituted for
beef.*

Sour Soup with Vegetables

แกงส้มผักรวม

Yield : 3 servings

2	tablespoons sour curry paste
7	(150 g.) shrimp, shelled and deveined
$1/2$	cup (80 g.) Chinese cabbage
$1/2$	cup (90 g.) white cabbage
$1/3$	cup (80 g.) white radish
$1/2$	cup (100 g.) string beans
$1^1/2$	cups stock

Seasoning

2	tablespoons fish sauce
1	tablespoon sugar
2	tablespoons lemon juice

Preparation

1. Bring the stock to the boil. Stir in the sour curry paste.
2. Cook the shrimp in the boiling stock mixture, add all the vegetables and the seasoning. Serve hot.

Note:
Various kinds of vegetables are recommended.

Chicken in Coconut Milk with Galangal

ต้มข่าไก่

Yield : 2 servings

½ cup (100 g.) chicken, boned and sliced
½ cup straw mushrooms, halved
1 piece galangal, thinly sliced
1 stalk lemongrass, cut into 1-inch pieces
3 kaffir lime leaves, shredded
1 tablespoon chillies, coarsely pounded
1 tablespoon coriander leaves
1½ cups thick coconut milk

Seasoning
3 tablespoons fish sauce
3 tablespoons lemon juice

Preparation
1. Pour the coconut milk into the pot, bring to a boil, add chicken and simmer for 5 minutes.
2. Add the straw mushrooms, galangal and lemongrass.
3. When boiled, add the seasoning and chillies. Serve hot in a bowl. Garnish with the kaffir lime leaves and coriander.

Mixed Meat Tom Yam Soup

ต้มยำรวมมิตร

Yield : 3 servings

5   *(90 g.) shrimp, shelled and deveined*
1   *(50 g.) squid, diagonally sliced and cut into pieces*
$^1/_4$ *cup (50 g.) pork, thinly sliced*
1   *tablespoon galangal, peeled and sliced*
1   *stalk lemongrass, cut into 1-inch pieces*
3   *kaffir lime leaves*
1   *tablespoon chillies, coarsely pounded*
2   *tablespoons coriander*
$^1/_2$ *cup (70 g.) straw mushrooms, halved*
1   *cup chicken stock*

Seasoning
2   *tablespoons fish sauce*
2   *tablespoons lemon juice*

Preparation
1. Bring the chicken stock to the boil, add the pork and seafood.
2. Simmer for 5 minutes, add all the seasoning.
3. Add the galangal, lemongrass, kaffir lime leaves, chillies and mushrooms.
4. When boiled, serve hot in the bowl garnished with coriander.

Spiced Beef Soup Country-Style

แกงป่าเนื้อ

Yield : 2 servings

2 tablespoons red curry paste
$1/2$ cup (100 g.) beef, thinly sliced
3 round eggplants, each cut into 4-6 pieces
$1/4$ cup (50 g.) string beans, cut into 1-inch pieces
3 kaffir lime leaves, shredded
$1/2$ cup coarsely shredded balsam leaves
2 red chillies
5 aromatic ginger (krachai) roots, finely chopped
2 cups stock

Seasoning
2 tablespoons fish sauce
1 teaspoon sugar

Preparation

1. Pour the stock into a saucepan, add the red curry paste. Bring to the boil.
2. Add the beef, simmer for 5 minutes.
3. Add the round eggplants, string beans, kaffir lime leaves and ginger roots. Bring to the boil again.
4. Add the seasoning and garnish with balsam leaves and chillies. Serve hot.

Note:
Pork may be substituted for beef.

Stir Fried Chicken with Cashew Nuts

ไก่ผัดเม็ดมะม่วง

Yield : 3 servings

$^1/_2$ cup (100 g.) chicken, cut into pieces
$^1/_2$ cup (150 g.) fried cashew nuts
$^1/_2$ (70 g.) onion, cut lengthwise
3 stalks spring onion, cut only the white into 1-inch pieces
2 tablespoons dried chillies, cut into 1-inch pieces and fried
3 tablespoons oil
$^1/_2$ cup chicken stock

Seasoning
1 tablespoon soy sauce
$^1/_2$ teaspoon thick soy sauce
1 teaspoon sugar
2 tablespoons oyster sauce
$^1/_4$ teaspoon ground pepper

Preparation
1. Heat the oil in a pan, add the chicken and stir for 5 minutes.
2. Add the cashew nuts, onion, spring onion, dried chillies, chicken stock and all the seasoning. Stir fry until heated through and serve hot.

Stir Fried Shrimp with Asparagus

กุ้งผัดหน่อไม้ฝรั่ง

Yield : 2 servings

7   (150 g.) shrimp, shelled and deveined
$1^{1}/_{2}$ cups (700 g.) asparagus, cut into 1-inch pieces
1   teaspoon garlic, finely chopped
3   tablespoons vegetable oil
$^{1}/_{2}$ cup chicken stock

Seasoning

1   tablespoon oyster sauce
1   teaspoon soy sauce
1   teaspoon sugar

Preparation

1. Heat the oil in a pan, fry the garlic until fragrant.
2. Add the shrimp and stir for 3 minutes.
3. Add the asparagus or broccoli, seasoning and chicken stock and bring to the boil. Transfer from the pan to a serving dish and serve hot.

Note:

Broccoli or cabbage may be substituted for the asparagus.

Mixed Vegetables with Shrimp

ผัดผักรวมมิตร

Yield : 2 servings

7   (150 g.) shrimp, shelled and
     deveined
1/2 cup (150 g.) carrots, thinly
     sliced crosswise
1/2 cup (110 g.) snow peas
1/2 cup (100 g.) Chinese cabbage
1   teaspoon garlic, finely chopped
3   tablespoon oil

Seasoning
1   teaspoon soy sauce
1   tablespoon oyster sauce
1/4 tablespoon ground pepper

Preparation
1. Heat the oil in a pan and fry the
   garlic until fragrant.
2. Add the shrimp. When cooked,
   add the vegetables and stir for
   5 minutes.
3. Add the seasoning and stir for
   another minute. Transfer to a
   serving dish and serve hot.

Note:
When cooking a variety of vegetables for the
same dish, put in the vegetables that are hard
to cook first so that all are ready at the same
time.

Beef with Oyster Sauce

เนื้อผัดน้ำมันหอย

Yield : 3 servings

1/2 cup (30 g.) pork or beef, cut into 1/2-inch pieces
1/4 cup onion, cut lengthwise
4 straw mushrooms, quartered
2 stalks spring onion, cut the white into 1-inch pieces
4 tablespoons oil
1 teaspoon garlic, finely chopped
1/4 cup stock
1 teaspoon tapioca flour or cornflour (cornstarch)

Seasoning

2 tablespoons oyster sauce
1 teaspoon soy sauce
1/4 teaspoon ground pepper

Preparation

1. Heat the oil in a pan, fry the garlic until fragrant. Add the beef and stir for 5 minutes.
2. Add the onion, straw mushrooms and spring onions. Add the stock.
3. Bring to the boil and add all the seasoning. Dissolve the flour with 2 tablespoons of water, pour the mixture into the pan and stir thoroughly. Serve hot.

Note:
Dried mushrooms can be substituted for straw mushrooms.

Stir Fried Hot and Spicy Pork

ผัดเผ็ดหมูสามชั้น

Yield : 3 servings

½ cup (100 g.) pork with fat, cut
    into thin cubes
2   tablespoons fresh green
    peppercorns
3   kaffir lime leaves
1   tablespoon aromatic ginger,
    finely chopped
3   tablespoons chilli paste
1   cup coconut milk
20 sweet basil leaves

Seasoning
2   tablespoons fish sauce
1   teaspoon sugar
¼   teaspoon ground pepper

Preparation
1. Pour the coconut milk into a
   heated pan, bring it to a boil
   for about 5 minutes, add the
   chilli paste, stir for 3 minutes
   until fragrant.
2. Add the pork until done. Stir in
   the seasoning. Mix in sweet
   basil leaves and serve.

- Three tablespoons of vegetable oil can be
  substituted for the coconut milk.
- The aromatic ginger is called krachai in
  Thai.

Eight Deities

ผัดโป๊ยเซียน

Yield : 3 servings

1   (20 g.) squid, diagonally slashed on each side and sliced

3   (30 g.) shrimp, shelled and deveined

1/4   cup (50 g.) pork, thinly sliced into 1-inch pieces

1/4   cup (50 g.) pork liver, thinly sliced

1/4   cup (50 g.) chicken breast, thinly sliced

1   tablespoon leeks, cut into 1/2-inch pieces

2   tablespoons spring onion, cut into 1/2-inch pieces

1/4   cup white cabbage, finely shredded

4   tablespoons vegetable oil

1   tablespoon cornflour (cornstarch)

1/4   cup chicken stock

Seasoning

3   tablespoons oyster sauce

1/4   teaspoon ground pepper

1   teaspoon seasoning sauce

1   teaspoon soy sauce

1   teaspoon sugar

Preparation

1. Heat 3 tablespoons of the oil in a pan, add all the meats and seafood, stir for 5 minutes.
2. Dissolve the cornflour in water, pour into the pan.
3. Add the seasoning, stir for another 2-3 minutes and set aside.
4. Wash the pan and heat 1 tablespoon of oil. Stir in the vegetables and chicken stock. Bring to the boil. Stir in the meat mixture. Serve hot.

Catfish with Fresh Peppercorn

ผัดปลาดุกพริกไทยอ่อน

Yield : 2 servings

1 cup (230 g.) catfish, cut into
   $^1/_2$- inch rounds
$^1/_2$ cup fresh peppercorn
1 tablespoon kaffir lime leaves
2 tablespoons sweet basil leaves
2 red and green chillies, cut into
   lengthwise
1 tablespoon garlic, finely chopped
4 tablespoons oil

Seasoning
2 tablespoons oyster sauce
1 tablespoon soy sauce
1 teaspoon ground pepper
1 tablespoon sugar
1 cup stock

Preparation
1. Cook catfish in boiling water, drain.
2. Heat saucepan with oil, fry garlic until fragrant, add catfish and stir for 3 minutes.
3. Add the fresh peppercorn, the seasoning and stock. Wait until it boils then add chillies, kaffir lime leaves and sweet basil. Serve hot.

Note:
Other fresh fish can be substituted for the catfish using the same method.

Stir Fried Shrimp with Coconut Palm Tip

ผัดกุ้งสดยอดมะพร้าวอ่อน

Yield : 3 servings

7   *(150 g) shrimp, shelled and deveined*
1   *cup (45 g) coconut tip, cut in 1x1 inch pieces*
2   *red or green chillies*
5   *stalks spring onion, cut only the white into 1-inch pieces*
3   *tablespoons vegetable oil*
$^1/_2$ *cup chicken stock*
1   *teaspoon garlic, finely chopped*

Seasoning

3   *tablespoons oyster sauce*
1   *teaspoon soy sauce*
$^1/_2$ *teaspoon sugar*
$^1/_4$ *teaspoon ground pepper*

Preparation

1. Heat the vegetable oil in a pan, add the chopped garlic and shrimp, stir for 3 minutes.
2. Add the coconut flesh, chicken stock and all the seasoning, bring to the boil. Add the chillies and spring onion. Serve hot and sprinkle with the ground pepper.

Note:
Before cooking, drain the coconut palm tip and rinse in hot water. Dry with a kitchen towel.

Stir Fried Thai Sausage with Eggs

ผัดแหนมกับไข่

Yield : 2 servings

3   small packages (90 g.) Thai
    sausages
1/2 (70 g.) onion, cut lengthwise
1   (70 g.) tomato, cut lengthwise
1   teaspoon garlic, finely chopped
2   stalks spring onion, cut the
    white into 1-inch pieces
2   chillies, sliced lengthwise
1   egg
3   tablespoons oil

Seasoning
1   tablespoon soy sauce
1   teaspoon sugar
1/4 teaspoon ground pepper

Preparation
1. Slice the Thai sausages
   diagonally.
2. Heat the oil in a pan, fry the
   garlic until fragrant. Add
   the beaten egg and stir for
   1 minute. Add the Thai
   sausages.
3. Add the vegetables and chillies.
4. Add the seasoning and stir
   thoroughly. Serve hot.

Mixed Sweet and Sour

ผัดเปรี้ยวหวานรวมมิตร

Yield : 3 servings

$^1/_4$ cup (50 g.) pork, thinly cut into 1/2-inch pieces

3 (100 g.) shrimp, shelled and deveined

$^1/_4$ cup squid, cut into crosswise 1-inch lengths

$^1/_2$ cup cucumber, cut diagonally

$^1/_2$ cup tomato, cut lengthwise

2 tablespoons spring onion, cut the white into 1-inch pieces

3 tablespoons onion, sliced lengthwise

1 teaspoon garlic, finely chopped

$^1/_2$ cup stock

3 tablespoons vegetable oil

Seasoning

1 tablespoon fish sauce

1 teaspoon sugar

2 tablespoons tomato sauce

Preparation

1. Heat the oil in a pan, fry the garlic until fragrant. Add the pork and seafood and stir for 3 minutes.
2. Add all the vegetables and stock, continue stirring.
3. When cooked, add the seasoning and transfer to a serving plate. Serve hot.

Note:

- *Other vegetables including baby corn and snow peas may be added or substituted for other vegetables.*
- *For thicker gravy, dissolve 2 tablespoons of tapioca flour or cornflour (cornstarch) in $^1/_4$ cup of water and add to the pan with the seasoning.*

Sweet and Sour Sea Bass

ผัดเปรี้ยวหวานปลากะพง

Yield : 3 servings

1	cup (500 g.) sea bass, cut into thick pieces
1	cup oil for deep frying the fish
1	cucumber, cut diagonally
3	pieces baby corn
5	pods of snow peas
1	small onion
1	tomato
2	tablespoons tapioca flour or cornflour (cornstarch)
$^1/_4$	cup oil
1	teaspoon garlic, finely chopped
$^1/_2$	cup stock

Seasoning

3	tablespoons tomato sauce
2	tablespoons fish sauce
1	tablespoon sugar

Preparation

1. Heat 1-cup oil in a pan and deep fry the fish. Remove fish and set aside.
2. Heat $^1/_4$ cup oil in a pan, fry the garlic until fragrant. Add all the vegetables and stir thoroughly for 2 minutes, then add the stock.
3. When cooked, add the deep fried fish, add the seasoning and transfer from the heat.

Roast Pork with Hot Sauce

หมูกรอบ

Yield : 2 servings

½ cup (125 g.) pork, thinly sliced lengthwise

Garnish
1 Chinese lettuce
1 tomato

Seasoning
1 tablespoon oyster sauce
1 teaspoon soy sauce
1 teaspoon sugar
½ teaspoon ground pepper

Preparation
1. Marinate the pork with the seasoning for 20 minutes. Grill the pork over low heat for 10-15 minutes or until golden brown.
2. Slice the grilled pork into strips. Transfer to a dish and decorate the dish with vegetables. Serve with the sauce.

Sauce
3 pickled garlic, finely chopped
3 shallots, finely chopped
3 chillies, finely chopped
5 coriander roots, finely chopped
1 teaspoon ground pepper
3 tablespoons lemon juice
1 tablespoon sugar
3 tablespoons fish sauce
1 teaspoon galangal, grilled and finely chopped
1 tablespoon tomato, roasted and chopped

Preparation of the sauce
Thoroughly mix all the ingredients in a bowl.

Steamed Prawns with Bean Vermicelli

กุ้งอบวุ้นเส้น

Yield : 3 servings

7	medium-sized prawns, shelled and deveined
1	cup bean vermicelli, soaked
2	stalks spring onion, cut into 1-inch pieces
1	piece ginger, thinly sliced
1	teaspoon roasted cumin
5	coriander stalks with roots

Seasoning

2	tablespoons oyster sauce
$1/4$	cup stock
1	tablespoon seasoning sauce
$1/2$	teaspoon ground pepper
2	stalks of coriander leaves, chopped

Preparation

1. Prepare a heavy flameproof casserole.
2. Put the ginger, cumin, coriander roots and spring onions in the casserole.
3. Add the prawns, bean vermicelli and seasonings. Cover the casserole.
4. Put the casserole over medium-low heat for 20-25 minutes. When done, sprinkle with the coriander leaves.

Omelette with Minced Pork

ไข่เจียวหมูสับ

Yield : 2 Servings

2　eggs
3　tablespoons (36 g.) ground pork
1　tablespoon onion, diced
1　tablespoon tomato, diced
1　tablespoon spring onion, finely chopped
1　cup oil

Seasoning

1　tablespoon soy sauce
$^1/_2$　teaspoon ground pepper
$^1/_2$　teaspoon sugar

Preparation

1. Mix all the ingredients together except the oil.
2. Add the seasoning and beat well.
3. Heat the oil in a pan over medium heat. Pour in the mixture and fry for 5 minutes.
4. Transfer from the pan and drain the oil. Serve hot.

Fancy Fried Eggs

ไข่ดาวทรงเครื่อง

Yield : 1 serving

1   egg
3   tablespoons onion, diced
3   tablespoons tomato, diced
1   cup oil for deep frying
$^1/_2$ cup (100 g.) ground pork
2   stalks coriander
1   teaspoon garlic, finely chopped

Seasoning

1   tablespoon fish sauce
2   tablespoons tomato sauce
1   tablespoon sugar
1   teaspoon lemon juice or vinegar
1   tablespoon soy sauce
$^1/_4$ cup stock

Preparation

1. Heat the oil in a pan, deep fry the egg and leave to cool.
2. Cut each fried egg into four quarters and transfer them to a serving plate.
3. In another pan, stir fry the garlic in four tablespoons of oil. Add the pork and continue stirring for about 2 minutes.
4. Add the tomato, onion and stir for another 2 minutes.
5. Pour in the stock and the seasoning, and bring to a boil.
6. Pour the sauce over the egg pieces and sprinkle with coriander leaves.

Grilled Pork

คอหมูย่าง

Yield: 5 servings

1   big piece (120 g.) pork, cut into
    ¹/₂ inch pieces
10 *barbecue sticks*

Seasoning
1   *teaspoon soy sauce*
1   *tablespoon oyster sauce*
¹/₄ *teaspoon ground pepper*
1   *teaspoon sugar*
1   *teaspoon seasoning sauce*
1   *teaspoon oil*

Garnish
Lettuce, tomato, cucumber

Preparation
1. Marinate the pork with the seasoning for 20-25 minutes.
2. Thread the meat onto the barbecue sticks. Grill the pork over medium heat for 10 minutes or until the pork is done.
3. Transfer the grilled pork to a serving dish and garnish with the vegetables.

Grilled Meatballs

ลูกชิ้นปิ้ง

Yield : 3 servings

25 meatballs (pork, chicken or beef)
5 wooden or barbecue sticks

Preparation

1. Cook the meatballs in boiling water for 1-2 minutes. Drain.
2. Thread the meatballs onto the wooden sticks. Grill over medium heat for 5 minutes.

Sauce

$^1/_2$ teaspoon salt
3 red chillies, chopped
2 tablespoons garlic
2 cloves of pickled garlic
$^1/_3$ cup vinegar
$^1/_3$ cup sugar

Preparation of the sauce

1. Mix all the ingredients together.
2. Simmer the mixture over medium heat for 25-30 minutes.

Three-Flavoured Fish

ปลาสามรส

Yield : 5 servings

1   (500 g.) fish
3   cups oil for deep frying
1   tablespoon coriander leaves
1   teaspoon salt

Seasoning
$^1/_4$ cup fish sauce
$^1/_4$ cup palm sugar
3   tablespoons tomato sauce
$^1/_4$ cup tamarind juice
3   red chillies
3   tablespoons small red chillies
5   tablespoons garlic, finely
     chopped
$^1/_4$ cup aromatic ginger

Preparation
1. Rub the salt all over the fish
   and leave for 10 minutes.
   Fry the fish over medium heat
   for about 15 minutes or until
   both sides are golden brown.
   Drain and transfer the fish to a
   serving plate. Set aside.
2. Blend all the seasoning
   together.
3. Pour the mixture on the fish
   and sprinkle with the coriander
   leaves. Serve immediately.

Hot and Sour Steamed Fish

ปลาช่อนแป๊ะซะ

Yield : 2 servings

1   (300 g.) fish
3   leaves of Chinese white cabbage
2   stalks Chinese celery, cut into
    1-inch pieces
1   red chillie, finely chopped
2   tablespoons ginger, finely
    chopped
5   pickled Chinese plums
2   tablespoons pickled plum juice
2   stalks spring onion, cut the
    white part into 1-inch pieces
2   cups stock

Seasoning
1   tablespoon fish sauce
1   tablespoon sugar
1   tablespoon seasoning sauce
1   tablespoon vinegar

Preparation
   Clean the fish and steam it over high heat for 20-25 minutes. Set aside.

Preparation of the sauce
1. Bring the stock to a boil, add the pickled plums and the plum juice.
2. Place the fish on a bed of Chinese cabbage in a flameproof bowl. Sprinkle with the celery, ginger, spring onions and red chilli.
3. Pour the stock on the fish and place the bowl over low heat, bring to a boil, add seasoning and serve.
4. Add more stock after serving if desired.

Crispy Fish with Chilli Sauce

ปลาเก๋าราดพริก

Yield: 5 servings

1   (500 g.) fish
3   cups oil for deep frying
1   tablespoon coriander leaves

Seasoning

$^1/_4$ cup fish sauce
$^1/_4$ cup palm sugar
$^1/_4$ cup tamarind juice
3   red chillies
3   tablespoons garlic
$^1/_4$ cup tomato sauce
3   tablespoons small red chillies

Preparation

1. Blend the seasoning in a blender or food processor. Set aside.
2. Score the fish by making diagonal slashes on each side.
3. Heat the oil in a pan. Deep fry the fish until both sides are golden brown.
4. Put the blended seasoning in no. 1 into a saucepan and simmer over low heat until the mixture is thick.
5. Before serving, pour the chilli sauce over the fish and sprinkle with the coriander leaves.

Note:
A deep fried fish does not stick to a pan if the pan and oil are hot and the fish is thoroughly sprinkled with salt.

Lime Pork

หมูมะนาว

Yield : 2 servings

1   cup (200 g.) pork
3   stalks Chinese kale
1   lime, cut into thin slices

Seasoning
3   tablespoons fish sauce
3   tablespoons lime juice
1   tablespoon garlic, finely chopped
1   tablespoon red chillies, finely chopped
1   tablespoon coriander, finely chopped
1   teaspoon sugar

Preparation
1. Grill the pork over medium-high heat until done.
2. Slice the pork thinly into large pieces. Transfer to a serving plate.
3. Remove the leaves of the Chinese kale, cut the stems into 1-inch pieces. Chill the kale stems for garnishing.
4. Thoroughly mix all the seasoning.
5. Pour the seasoning mixture on the pork. Garnish with lime slices and kale stems. Serve immediately.

Stuffed Omelette

ไข่ยัดไส้

Yield : 1 serving

1   egg
1   tablespoon tomato, diced
1   tablespoon onion, diced
1   tablespoon string beans, finely
      chopped
1   tablespoon peas
1   tablespoon straw mushrooms,
      diced
$^1/_4$ cup oil
$^1/_2$ cup (100 g.) ground pork
2   stalks coriander
1   red chilli, sliced lengthwise
1   teaspoon garlic, finely chopped
$^1/_4$ cup stock

Seasoning

1   tablespoon soy sauce
1   tablespoon fish sauce
1   tablespoon oyster sauce
$^1/_2$ teaspoon ground pepper
1   tablespoon sugar
1   tablespoon tomato sauce

Preparation

1. Heat a small amount of oil in a pan.
2. Beat the egg and add 1 teaspoon of water. Beat well.
3. Pour the beaten egg into the pan and spread the egg over low heat to make a thin sheet. When done, remove the egg sheet from the pan.
4. In another pan, heat the remaining oil and add the garlic. Stir fry until the garlic is fragrant, add the onion, tomato, string beans, peas and mushrooms. Stir well, then pour in the stock and bring to the boil. Add the seasoning, stir until the mixture is dry. Leave to cool.
5. Put the mixture onto the middle of the egg sheet. Fold the egg sheet into a square. Garnish with coriander leaves and red chilli slices.

Dancing Prawns

กุ้งเต้น

Yield : 2 servings

1   *(140 g.) big prawn*
1   *tablespoon lemongrass, finely chopped*
1   *tablespoon galangal, thinly sliced*
1   *tablespoon coriander root, finely chopped*
1   *tablespoon small red chillies, finely chopped*
1   *tablespoon rice, roasted and finely crushed*
1   *tablespoon mint leaves*

Seasoning
3   *tablespoons lemon juice*
2   *tablespoons fish sauce*
$^1/_2$ *teaspoon sugar*

Preparation

1. Grill the prawn until its shell turns light brown or for about 5 minutes. Shell the prawn and place it on a serving dish.
2. Mix the lemongrass, ginger, coriander root, red chillies and rice powder together. Add all the seasoning and stir well.
3. Pour the sauce over the prawn and sprinkle with the mint leaves.

Grilled Chicken and Sticky Rice

ข้าวเหนียวไก่ย่าง

Yield : 1 serving

1/2   *cup sticky rice*
2   *cups water*
1   *piece of thin white cloth*
3   *chicken thighs*

Seasoning
1   *tablespoon soy sauce*
1   *tablespoon oyster sauce*
$^1/_2$ *teaspoon ground pepper*
1   *tablespoon seasoning sauce*
$^1/_2$ *teaspoon sugar*

Vegetables for a side dish
Cabbage, Chinese white cabbage, string beans.

Preparation of the sticky rice
1. Rinse and drain the sticky rice twice. Soak the sticky rice in water for 2 hours.
2. Rinse and drain again.
3. Lay the cloth inside a steamer, bring the steamer to a boil. Sprinkle the sticky rice on the cloth and steam for 10 minutes. Stir the sticky rice gently and continue steaming for another 10 minutes or until done.

Preparation of the chicken
1. Marinate the chicken with the seasoning and leave for 30 minutes.
2. Grill the chicken over low heat until brown or done.

Note:
The grilled chicken may be served with sauce. To prepare the sauce, mix 1 tablespoon of chilli powder, 1 tablespoon of fish sauce and $^1/_2$ tablespoon of lemon juice. The sticky rice is cooked when it is transparent.

Pork Satay

หมูสะเต๊ะ

Yield : 2 servings

2   *cups (400 g.) pork with fat,*
cut into serving pieces about
¹/₂-inch thick
10   *satay sticks*

Seasoning
2   *tablespoons sugar*
1   *tablespoon curry powder*
1   *tablespoon soy sauce*
1   *tablespoon oyster sauce*
1   *tablespoon seasoning sauce*

Satay sauce
1   *cup (240 g.) thick coconut milk*
3   *tablespoons roasted peanuts,*
ground
1   *teaspoon curry powder*
2   *tablespoons sugar*
1   *tablespoon fish sauce*
¹/₂   *teaspoon salt*

Cucumber dip
1   *cup vinegar*
1¹/₂ *cups sugar*
2   *tablespoons salt*
5   *cucumbers, quartered and thinly*
sliced
2   *red chillies, cut into pieces*
4   *shallots, thinly sliced*

Preparation of the pork
1. Mix the pork with all the seasoning. Marinate for ¹/₂ hour.
2. Thread the pork onto the satay sticks.

Preparation of the satay sauce
1. Bring the coconut milk to the boil, add the seasoning.
2. Add the salt and curry powder, stir until the sauce is thick.
3. Shortly before transferring the mixture from the heat, add the peanuts and mix well.

Preparation of the cucumber dip
1. Mix the vinegar, sugar and salt together over low heat until the sugar and salt are dissolved. Leave to cool.
2. When served, add cucumbers, shallots and chillies to the vinegar mixture.

Note:
Beef or chicken may be substituted for pork

Leaf-Wrapped Chicken

ไก่ห่อใบเตย

Yield: 3 servings

10   *pandanus (toey) leaves*
1   *cup (250 g.) chicken, cut into*
     1 x 1 inch cubes
3   *cups oil*

Seasoning

1   *tablespoon soy sauce*
1   *tablespoon seasoning sauce*
1   *teaspoon sugar*
$^1/_2$ *teaspoon ground pepper*
1   *teaspoon oyster sauce*

Preparation

1. Mix the chicken with the seasoning. Marinate for half an hour.
2. Wrap each piece of marinated chicken with a pandanus leaf in a triangular shape.
3. Heat the oil over medium heat, deep fry the wrapped chicken. Drain the oil and serve.

Note:
Greaseproof paper may be substituted for the pandanus leaves.

Sticky Rice with Mangoes

ข้าวเหนียวมะม่วง

Yield : 3 servings

2 cups (400 g.) sticky rice
2 cups (480 g.) thick coconut milk
1 cup sugar
1 teaspoon salt
3 ripe mangoes, cut crosswise into thick pieces
1 tablespoon mung beans, toasted
1 tablespoon cornstarch (cornflour)

Seasoning

1½ cups thick coconut milk
1 cup sugar
½ teaspoon salt

Preparation

1. Rinse and drain the sticky rice twice. Soak the sticky rice in water for 3-5 hours.
2. In a double steamer, bring the water to the boil. Lay a piece of thin white cloth over the upper steamer and put in a few pandanus leaves to make the sticky rice fragrant. Put the rice on the cloth.
3. Steam for 15 minutes. Open the steamer and turn the sticky rice over with a ladle. Steam for another 10 minutes.
4. Boil the seasoning over medium heat. When boiled, drain through a piece of white cloth. Leave to cool.
5. Put the hot sticky rice into the sauce (No. 4), stir together well. Cover for 1 hour or until the sticky rice cools to room temperature.
6. Mix the 2 cups of coconut milk with the salt, sugar and cornstarch, bring to the boil. Drain through a piece of white cloth. This sauce is for topping.
7. Put the sticky rice and mangoes on a serving dish. Pour the topping sauce over the sticky rice and sprinkle with the toasted mung beans.

Note:
The sticky rice must be warm (not hot) when served. The mango should be chilled.

Sticky Rice with Durian in Coconut Milk

ข้าวเหนียวทุเรียน

Yield : 4 servings

1   cup (180 g.) durian meat
1   cup sticky rice
2   cups thick coconut milk
1   cup sugar
1   teaspoon salt
1   tablespoon sugar

Preparation

1. Method for the sticky rice, see the previous recipe (Sticky Rice with Mangoes).
2. Dissolve $1/2$ cup of the coconut milk, sugar and $1/2$ teaspoon of salt over medium heat. Add $1/2$ cup of the durian meat, keep the other half for garnishing.
3. The coconut milk topping comprises: $1/2$ cup of coconut milk, 1 tablespoon of sugar and $1/2$ teaspoon of salt. Mix them over medium heat and drain through a piece of white cloth.
4. Transfer the sticky rice to a bowl, top it with durian meat. Pour a small portion of the coconut milk onto the sticky rice.

Bananas in Sweet Coconut Milk

กล้วยบวชชี

Yield : 4 servings

5   firm bananas
2¹/₂ cups coconut milk
¹/₂ cup sugar
¹/₂ teaspoon salt
1   tablespoon sesame seeds, toasted

Preparation

1. Peel the bananas, split them lengthwise and cut each half into 4 pieces.
2. In a saucepan, bring 2 cups of the coconut milk to the boil, drop in the bananas, boil again then add sugar. Set aside.
3. For the topping, mix ¹/₂ cup of the coconut milk and ¹/₂ teaspoon of salt over low heat until the mixture is dissolved. Do not bring it to the boil. Set aside.
4. Transfer the bananas and coconut milk to a bowl, pour on the topping and sprinkle with the toasted sesame seeds.

Note:
Use yellowish green, not ripe and not completely raw bananas.

Bananas in Syrup

กล้วยเชื่อม

Yield : 2 servings

5   yellowish green bananas
1   cup coconut cream
$^1/_2$ teaspoon salt

Syrup
1   cup water
$^1/_2$ cup sugar
1   teaspoon lemon juice

Preparation

1. Warm the coconut milk over low heat. Do not bring to the boil. Add salt and set aside.
2. In a saucepan, mix the water and sugar over low heat. Bring to the boil and add the lemon juice. Peel the bananas and put them into the saucepan one at a time.
3. Simmer over low heat for about 5 minutes.
4. Transfer the bananas to a serving plate and pour over them the coconut milk mixture.

Note:
- *The lemon juice in the syrup makes the bananas appear shiny.*
- *Peel the bananas immediately before putting them in the syrup, or they will turn black.*
- *For thicker coconut cream, add a mixture of 2 teaspoons of cornstarch and water into the cream.*

Rice Flour Strings in Coconut Cream

ปลากริมไข่เต่า

Yield : 4 servings

1½ cups rice flour
2 tablespoons sticky rice flour
3 cups water
1 cup thick coconut milk
1 cup thin coconut milk
½ teaspoon salt
1 cup palm sugar

Preparation

1. Mix the rice flour and sticky rice flour with water. Knead to a stiff dough. Shape teaspoonfuls of the dough into pencil-like strings about 1-inch long by rolling in both palms.
2. Boil the water and toss in the flour strings. Transfer from the boiling water when the strings are cooked and float on the surface. Rinse through cool water, drain.
3. Divide the dough into half, one for the salty portion and the other for the sweet portion.

Preparation of the salty portion

In a saucepan, mix one half of the flour strings with the thick coconut milk and salt over low heat. When boiled, transfer from the heat.

Preparation of the sweet portion

In another saucepan, mix the other half of the flour strings with the thin coconut milk and palm sugar over low heat. When boiled, transfer from the heat.

While serving, put equal amounts of the two portions into a serving bowl.

Black Beans and Tapioca Balls

ถั่วดำสาคูเปียก

Yield : 4 - 5 servings

1 cup (170 g.) tapioca pellets
1 cup (150 g.) black beans
1¹/₂ cup sugar
2¹/₂ cup thick coconut milk
¹/₂ teaspoon salt
1 cup water

Preparation

1. In a saucepan, bring the water to the boil. Rinse the tapioca pellets and toss into the water. Stir continuously until done or until the white pellets turn transparent. Add ¹/₂ cup of the sugar, stir together well. Set aside.

2. Rinse the black beans, soak in water for 3 hours and drain. Boil the beans in water over low heat until cooked. Remove from the heat and drain.

3. In another saucepan, mix the coconut milk with sugar and place over the heat. Add the beans and bring to the boil. Transfer from the heat. Set aside.

4. In a small saucepan, warm ¹/₂ cup of the coconut milk and ¹/₂ teaspoon of the salt over low heat. Do not bring to the boil. Remove from heat.

5. To serve, put a spoonful of the tapioca pellets into a serving bowl, pour over the black beans (No. 3) and the coconut milk (No.4).

Coconut Jelly

วุ้นมะพร้าวอ่อน

Yield : 4 servings

1   cup (100 g.) soft coconut meat,
    grated
1   tablespoon gelatine powder
2   cups water
1   cup sugar

Coconut cream
1   cup thick coconut milk
1   teaspoon salt

Preparation

1. Dissolve the gelatine powder
   with the water over low heat.
   Add the sugar and stir
   continuously for 7-10 minutes.
   Add the coconut meat and
   simmer.
2. In another saucepan, warm the
   coconut milk and salt over low
   heat. Do not bring to the boil.
   Set aside.
3. Mix No.1 and No. 2 together
   well. Pour the mixture into
   prepared moulds. Leave to
   cool.

Chestnut Cubes in Coconut Milk

ทับทิมกรอบ

Yield : 4 servings

1 cup tapioca flour
1 cup (150 g.) diced water chestnuts
1 cup red syrup
1 cup sugar
3 whole water chestnuts
2¹/₂ cups water
1 cup thick coconut milk
¹/₂ teaspoon salt
  crushed ice

Preparation of the water chestnut cubes

1. Soak the diced water chestnuts in the red syrup for 30 minutes, or until water chestnuts become red. Drain.
2. Put the tapioca flour in a bowl, toss in the red water chestnuts until the chestnut cubes are coated with the flour. Set aside.
3. Bring 2 cups of the water to the boil. Drop in the flour-coated chestnut cubes. Transfer the chestnut cubes when cooked or floating on the surface. Rinse in cold water. Drain.

Preparation of the coconut milk syrup

1. Bring ¹/₂ cup of the water to the boil, Add sugar, simmer over low heat until the sugar is dissolved. Transfer from the heat and put the three whole water chestnuts in the syrup. Set aside.
2. In another saucepan, mix the coconut milk and salt over low heat. Do not bring to the boil. Set aside.
3. Put a portion of the water chestnuts and syrup in a serving bowl. Add the coconut milk and crushed ice. Serve immediately.

Pumpkin Custard

สังขยาฟักทอง

Yield : 2 servings

1   (500 g.) pumpkin
5   eggs
1   cup thick coconut milk
1   cup sugar
5   pandanus leaves

Preparation

1. Slice across the top of the pumpkin. Scrape out the spongy pith with seeds to make a hole about 5 inches in diameter.
2. Rinse the pumpkin and drain.
3. Mix the eggs, coconut milk and sugar thoroughly. Squeeze the pandanus leaves to produce juice and add the juice to the mixture (or use an electric mixer to beat the ingredients for 5 minutes). Drain and set aside.
4. Boil water in a double steamer, put the pumpkin into the top of the steamer and pour the mixture in No. 3 into the pumpkin.
5. Steam over medium heat for about 30 minutes. Leave to cool before removing the pumpkin from the steamer.

Note:
To prevent the pumpkin from cracking:
- *Put the pumpkin into a bowl that fits it exactly.*
- *Do not steam over high heat.*
- *Do not immediately remove the steamed pumpkin from the steamer. Leave it to cool.*

Wandee Na Songkhla

One of Thailand's culinary experts, Wandee na Songkhla has been a veteran lecturer in home economics and Thai cooking at various institutes. She is the author of several Thai cookbooks including two extensively-researched books on *"Royal Thai Cuisine"* of the olden days as mentioned in the literature written by King Rama II and King Rama VI.

After years of research, she also wrote another book on *"Royal Favourite Dishes"*, based on the *"Hungry Diary"* — a memoir of King Rama V during his journey to Europe in 1897.

She was an honorary member of the editorial team for a royally-initiated encyclopaedia for Thai youths, concentrating on the chapter on Thai food. She has from time to time demonstrated the techniques of Thai cooking on television and in international food exhibitions in such major cities as Houston, Denver, New York, Hong Kong and Tokyo.

She has in the last several years been a specialist teacher on traditional Thai food at the royally-founded Tamnak Suan Kularb College in Bangkok.

Index

Banana
Bananas in Sweet Coconut Milk **166**
Bananas in Syrup **169**

Beef
Sun-Dried Beef **20**
Fried Rice with Salted Beef **31**
Spiced Beef Salad *(Yam Neua Yang)* **71**
Spicy Beef/Fork Salad *(Lab Neua/Mu)* **77**
Hot and Sour Beef Soup **91**
Spiced Beef Soup Country-Style **101**
Beef with Oyster Sauce **111**

Black Beans
Black Beans with Tapioca Balls **174**

Chicken
Fried Rice with Chicken and Mint Leaves **33**
Chicken in Coconut Milk with Galanga **97**
Stir Fried Chicken with Cashew Nuts **105**
Grilled Chicken and Sticky Rice **153**
Leaf-Wrapped Chicken **156**

Coconut
Coconut Jelly **177**
Chestnut Cubes in Coconut Milk **179**

Crab
Stuffed Crab **19**
Crab Nuggets **27**
Fried Rice with Crabmeat **39**

Duck
Roast Duck Curry **86**

Egg
Omelette with Minced Pork **132**
Fancy Fried Eggs **135**
Stuffed Omelette **148**

Fish
Fried Fish and Mango Salad **69**
Catfish Flakes Salad **73**
Sour Soup with Fish **93**
Catfish with fresh Peppercorn **116**
Sweet and Sour Seabass **124**
Three-Flavoured Fish **140**
Hot and Sour Steamed Fish **143**
Crispy Fish with Chilli Sauce **145**
Shrimp Paste Dip with Catfish Flakes **159**

Noodle
Crispy Noodles **17**
Pan-Fried Noodles with Pork and
    Asparagus **47**
Pan-Fried Noodles with Chicken **49**
Noodles Fried with Spicy Chicken **50**
Tom Yam Shrimp Noodles Soup *(Spicy
    Shrimp Noodle Soup)* **53**
Pan-Fried Spicy Noodles **55**
Phat Thai Kung Sod *(Stir-Fried Thai
    Noodles with Shrimp)* **57**
Fried Noodles with Shrimp, Vegetables
    and Gravy **58**
Steamed Prawns with Bean Vermicelli **131**

Papaya
Green Papaya Salad 79

Pork
Pork Toast 12
Rice Crackers with Dip 23
Thick Curry with Pork 83
Stir Fried Hot and Spicy Pork 113
Roast Pork with Hot Sauce 129
Grilled Pork 137
Grilled Meatballs 139
Lime Pork 147
Pork Satay 155

Prawn
Dancing Prawns 151

Pumpkin
Pumpkin Custard 181

Rice Flour
Rice Flour Pudding with Sweet Eggs 171
Rice Flour Strings in Coconut Cream 173

Sausage
Fried Rice with Sausage 34
Fried Rice with Chinese Sausage 41
Fried Rice with Thai Sausage 42
Stir Fried Thai Sausage with Eggs 121

Seafood
Spiced Seafood and Meat Salad 65
Mixed Meat Tom Yam Soup 99
Eight Dieties 115
Sweet and Sour Meat 123

Shrimp
Spring Rolls 15
Shrimp Nuggets 25
Fried Rice with Shrimp 37
Spicy Shrimp Salad 74
Green Curry with Shrimp 85
Tom Yam Kung 89
Stir Fried Shrimp with Asparagus 107
Stir Fried Shrimp with Coconut Palm Tip 119

Squid
Spiced Squid Salad 63

Sticky Rice
Sticky Rice with Mangoes 163
Sticky Rice with Durian in Coconut Milk 16

Vegetable
Sour Soup with Vegetables 94
Mixed Vegetables with Shrimps 108

Vermicelli
Bean Vermicelli Salad 66
Steamed Prawns with Bean Vermicelli 131